THE AMATEUR SCIENTIST'S NOTEBOOK

The Amateur Scientist's Notebook

Poems

Jesse DeLong

BAOBAB PRESS

RENO, NV

First Printing

ISBN-13: 978-1-936097-36-4
ISBN-10: 1-936097-36-2

Library of Congress Control Number: 2020949225

Baobab Press
121 California Ave
Reno, Nevada 89509
www.baobabpress.com

To my family, for everything.

Contents

Experiments in the Field of Light

"Because of the altitude, or the damp, or the kind of grass that grew in such places, they were radiant, smoldering, gold with transparency, accepting light all together. Thousands of florets . . ."

—Marilynne Robinson, "Psalm Eight"

Florets

1.

The struggle of scale begins
in a sunflower. Floret: sharp of petals, stem-bright,

it starts—to fill air, to feed earth, to forge,
from root to flower,

the color & coarseness of its borders while around sprouts
the collage of a larger order. Feathers, flora,

> Bird, I light a lamp,
> wick submitted to
> kerosene. A horizon of
> dust furrows. Restless, I
> withhold any offerings
> as you settle into the sofa—
> a sunflower plucked
> & lain on pink clovers.

phosphorus, water & light. A sunflower
bound of small flowers blooming in the sun.

What is one is once lost.
Torn, once lost in one
empties into soil

> Bird, you inherit such gestures:
> Sand releasing its shape to water.
> A cloud bruising in leaflets of rain.

into the toil of root fibers
curling around a ribcage, minerals measuring the level of

> Our difference—
> a chrysanthemum-colored bee,
> a drone, carraging no spores, no
> stinger, no home.

light absorption on a leaf. Simply split,
the strewn can be supported by the order. Feathers, flora.

A lamp sprouts
through the air. Slowly
you rise. You are the bulb I was
born to close my eyes to.
I try
to touch
your arm, but you are
already in the bathroom.
In the mirror, I
memorize you
massaging soap on
your fingers.

Or to say our ozone is one
big lungful of air where particles of leaf, litter,
& clay collide in the fringes of tissue.

2.

tissues of song,
    of sinew, wind, & root.

3.

Sallow as moth wings, I stare.
Clouds rattle the sky like dust

in a furnace. Nothing
is perfect. I spent the morning

sorting through every door you'd entered.
Feeling powder fluttering in my chest, I

step outside where you are
reading haibun under the house's shade

& grass is muttering
a language too green for glare.

The chrysanthemums
keep sunlight in little boxes

on their petals.
What is the contour

taken in the brain
when restlessness finally

subsides? You

set the book aside & sleep
with a hat over your eyes.
The sunflowers begin

to napkin-up the light,
rice paper between my fingers.

>Vapors
>on soil, centers
>rough
>as wristlines. I
>delicately rotate
>their bodies,
>careful not to
>tremble, wary
>even of my
>own
>breath.

4.

For those sunflowers of May, clarity strikes
everything a petal or stem displays, a revelation

by route of pigmentation, or the scriptures of shade
composed in vein on undergrowth. Thousands of florets,

>I light a fire beside the river
>to crave the shade your face keeps.
>The sky tarnished in smoke, flames & ash.
>When you grace the bank, lungs lit,
>water drumming a tune blood knows,
>I announce the night
>our god, no wind, no,
>the moment, no
>moment.

so tiny they squander intricacy on light cherished,
smoldering, gold with transparency, canvassing

petal-centers in the borderlines
of hunger. Everything the soil supports

is foreseen in seed. The land
lying out before summer like an exhalation.

A single floret of smoke points onward.

Floret as Water

Crisp in the lungs, Autumn then is a breath
held. Stems begin to brittle. Birds forage for seeds.
Coyote bones: white waste on the river's red bank.

    Broadcasts lost in snow,
    we drive the interstate where time is
    suspended between long purple shadows
    & morning when the birds bleat. Sleeping, &
    the warmth of your breath gathers on glass.
    When I stir, you smile, staring
    to where fronds of headlights are guiding
    us home. The gap between pure white & pure
    black the axis our bodies rotate. When I
    turn, your eyes are closed.
    Scribbled in fog is the word *we.*

What is a bone bleached in riverlight if I am
always restless, & restless enough to scavenge
(a chickadee sings somewhere in the snow-
covered trees, its voice a whistle & whistle's echo,
the moth dead on the windowsill for days) for those
who tire to scrape throats through frost?

    Snow sloshes the lawn—
    pebbles, mud, & ice-chunks.
    A sparrow docks
    on the fencepost, ruffles
    water from wings. Ah, the sun
    again. I light
    near the snow globe you gifted me
    during a softer winter. The glass is chipped
    & eclipses a ring on the windowsill's
    dry wood. In stained fingers,
    sky mirrors on the crest
    of the globe, clouds swell, the bird
    shadows its wings upside down in departure.

Dusk in a tree, slowly,
slowly. The sky an ice-
stilled atom where a brown bat skreels,
ultrasonic in the cooling air. I want to

pronounce the distance,
                    rattle the treble-point where space
& time collide.   Materials of lung & liver
etched in this layer:
                    Where one is one, & once lost in one.

   Where one is once   here & there. The imprint
our bodies make on autumn & after.

        Past the globe,
        land emerges in chalklines, a spine
        of hills narrowing to knuckles, ridges sharpened
        where the sky has lit its paper ends. If only
        our rituals really nourished us.

Near the river-dawn, I tender, as if anything more,
the coyote rib. Morning slates on
pebbles. The current disassembles the sun.

        Roadlights the only sound
        in the room. The curtains could be
        the northern lights. The carpet
        a tar pit. This is the void
        I willingly enter
        every day. I cross
        my arms, rest my hands
        at my shoulders.
        Fingers spread, I
        take a step
        back, a step forward, a
        step back
        & to the
        side.

Some ants march from a fallen tree to where an apple core
browns on weeds. The hunger goes on

& on like this. An animal
knowing from which flares of love you feed.

Occurrence of Phosphorous Intermediates in Florets

Where Observed	Intermediates	Florets, Referents of
Potato Tubers	Irises Uprooted	My father cleft his hands into the soil. It was noon, 1975. He'd ridden on a train
Oat Seedlings	Trainlight digging up what lies ahead	for four hours & walked a dirt road home, irises picketed along the ditch. The sun pressed a sack of oats on his shoulders. Wounded by his fingers, earth emitted the pheromones of a horse after its rider first settles into saddle. From the dirt, he removed a tuber & held it like he would the weight of his son's head. He placed the tuber in the center of his kitchen table, beside a horse-tail braid of irises. As he walked towards the barn, his path cleft through the clover field. Bats in the rafters. Sunlight sporing through the stable's slats, ox-blood colored, hay-dust solar as upcoming railings. From a burlap sack, he tendered oats in his palm, & the horse cleft its lips into the seedlings, my father rubbing its neck, minutes later working dirt from a potato's skin under the faucet.
Grapes	A nail arched from a long finger	My mother walked into a carpet of clover, stems arching on her ankles like purring
Legume Seeds		cats. She carried grapes in an egg-white handkerchief, & kneeled & set the bundle on a mat of flora, carefully stretching every corner so the handkerchief became a tablecloth & the grapes a feast. A ladybug lighted on a clover, its red body gemmed. Years earlier, while still young enough to ruby carelessly in sunlight, she ran (red earrings winged) beside a fence where grapes grew, rattling her fingers through the soft marbles of fruit. Hidden below a curtain of leafs, a nail split her thumb (the same way, in the clover patch, she would puncture grape skins). A single drop of blood ladybugged on a leaf.

Sedum Leafs

Beets, Spinach-
   Leafs &
      Petioles

The pressure
of night
fall

In a meadow, my
mother &
old man,
maybe not so
old at this time,
spread out a quilt &
lay under the silk-
screen shade
of clouds.
Inside the woven
basket, carried like
a tacklebox,
were beets, chard
coated in olive
oil, garlic
& goat cheese.
A large mason jar
filled with water &
a few cucumber slices
for flavor. When
they finished
eating, he dumped
his eyes like a pile
of earth on her.
Lying on her
stomach, one leg
raised,
her toenails
offered up the sky,
& she stared at stonecrop
flowers draped under
the weight of last night's
light rain. Certain breeds'
petioles could be
mixed with kale
to give the meal a taste
of tea & old
earth. Others
could clutch lungs
to rawhide
& I knew,
from what she'd admitted,
she carried both with her.
When he was picking potatoes,
she felt roots shuffling sand in her lungs,
though, some days, when he left for the

field,
five flowering stonecrop fingers sprouted,
their stamens resting stations for lady-
bugs.
She always wanted to or always would be
affected by a field of different-
colored florets. A giant raindrop
of light spelunked through the trees:
irises & blue grass &
sedum leafs beaming—
glass blown
from a streetlamp.

Pea Seedlings

Tea Leaves

Trout &
vegetables in
green broth

In a porcelain bowl, a pile of pea pods lay like the bloated husks of mantises. Flecks earthed the rim's gloss. My parents' fingers were smeared in dirt & they'd already filled several plastic bags full enough to balloon the linings. Through the kitchen window, sunlight on the kettle cast a caterpillar-bright reflection. Anchored by spoons, tea bags soiled the water to the murk of pond-silt flicked up by a trout. They fished out the tea bags & deposited them on the bank of the bowl. Sunlight gave over to more sunlight. Yesterday at the pond's edge, I watched you strain your arms, pole bent like a rain-heavy stonecrop. When you reeled, you used the same motion as my mother stirring heated milk into tea. The trout fought hard before surrendering to the warmer flesh of my palms & must have broken the water in a similar startle as pea sprouts rupturing through soil. We lay the fish on the bank, & I split its belly, later splitting pea pods, boiling them both with a handful of tea bags, eating this meal my father shared with me for a few days with you.

Sunflowers

Grapefruit
Pulp

A row of
stalks
lain out like
railings

With your long red
thumbnail, you
puncture a grapefruit &
un-shell like strips of thick
paper its peelings.

The pulp, padded
like the body of
a caterpillar, spouts
down your wrist
a silken thread
of juice.
A tea kettle songbirds—
the sound of a train riding
the acid railings
of midnight, always
at midnight when our thoughts
first un-floret
to dream. We carry
the tea & grapefruit outside.
The sky is wrung grey in wind.
The pines are tattered
scarecrows on the horizon.
The houses light
up, sudden as lily pads
crushed by a man wading in
after a trout. We root
our hands in soil
cold as a teabag left
in an empty cup.
Past where the clovers
quilt, our horse is
eating oats
in the barn,
his breath
rising to the plume
of florets the train
arrives with for us
always & always
at midnight.

Newton & the Law of Grave Eating

Picture Newton as an older boy, almost a man. This would be during some summer at his family's farm in Woolsthorpe. While he was digging an irrigation ditch, he noticed a girl amble up the road, holding a parcel of letters & a package wrapped in brown paper. When she neared him, she rested beside three makeshift graves. The headstones were crossed with poplar limbs, the joints strengthened with twine. From the paper, the girl unwrapped an apple. As Isaac strained under the meeting strengths of shovel & earth, he watched her eat the fruit to its core. When she finished, she allowed their eyes to meet & placed the core on top of the grave & continued up the road. A few days later Newton wandered under an oak tree, brooding over this equation: how a person (say, a girl) can be propelled by her own force of duty, like a stone thrown across a field, & how, at the same time, she can be lured by another (say, a young ditch digger) the way the rock eventually falls to grass. If the force she is lured to, Isaac thought, is stronger than the force she is propelled from, then like the rock she will get caught up by grave eating. Though, if the force the girl propels toward carries forward in her mind while at the same time the force she is attracted to continues diverting her, then she will carry both forwards & downwards, both away from him & towards him, suspended in perpetual, bewildering motion.

Floret as Phosphorus

Oxygen blackmails the glow, a low, natural
radiance for rock & skin cells. Though there are separate

damages from the phosphor of fluorescent lamps
to the over-bright smolder
of shins sparking pale to pale on grass.

    Keen: a sharp edge or very eager perception.
    As in, a bird, once traveled across the continent,
    recalls forever those same strains
    of muscle. Memory as an energy rewoven.

    Keen: to lament or wail for (the dead).
    As in, a man holds—
    among other survivors—
    her skin & cotton sheets
    before she wants to be
    bird, wrists pinned, him
    swallowing the blue
    blotch in her eye-white,
    of their eyes, her eyes, theirs,
    pupils flickering, lids quickening,
    in orgasm.

Though   (if I must call you bird)
if I must say, if I must,

                    flesh provides

more filler than feathers, however skin recognizes
its reliance on the scale from lantern-shine to shade:
the burn it must endure
                to be or not be   bird.

We situate between the bright flicker of man & woman.
We retreat into the duskiness where pheromones emit.

Wearing grey overalls & no shirt
a man wades into the river's open cells.
He scopes a sundress
snagged in reeds,
sunflowers patterning white cotton:
darkened from crawdads & clay.

Come, Bird—If skin, stone, feather or bone
wrests from phosphorus
                                        a shadow
(a white flag in water, a marker of grass where bodies grate)
then we must admit the blue moth of flame—us

> Under the outside spigot, I tip
> a clear plastic jug,
> turn the nozzle, & watch
> a moth ruffle into the container.

> Every day, the moth nests in the cooled air
> of the pipe, slurping the remnants

> of drainage. She finds herself urged to the wall—
> pressure, oxygen & silt—
> wings beating toward the light
> she tried so hard to hide from.

                        *

> In this version, you are the moth.
> In others, it's me. How can we make

> the corrections we need to, like a person wanting—
> because of injuries occurred & the moth's trapped state—

> to remedy another, when, in rescuing,
> we rasp from wings the powder which gives her height.

the solar sear a star plasmas
its chemicals on air, the electric electric.

See, a man steps into the net of lamplight.
He holds a glass of water at the carapace

of his belly. The scent of him, like paper
burned up & left in rain, looms.

> The man lays out the dress's material
> on the riverbank. On red earth cotton presses
> like a map where routes are scored
> in burn marks & the aftertaste
> of supermarket perfume. He says
> these mountains (ridges rote from leaf
> to leaf) allude to flesh

& quills. She will be remembered
more than a neckline welcome as dirt
roads, the times townsmen fucked
their wives like sparrows & thought of her
abrading feathers.

A woman attends to a paper lantern powdering on grass.
She knows light diminishing—
the over-bright of what it is propelled from
                    dies out until it arrives
                        at what it is propelled towards—
is how one locates in the world.

Stepping into the pine-scented pungency

of a man's sweat, she either concedes
her own perspiration or possesses it.

A woman carries the paper lantern
into the woods until its white wings are swallowed.

A man, attracted to a moth in a jar,
shatters not the glass which hoards the insect's small breaths,

but opens the lid & liberates it of its wings.
A woman watches, horrified, but holding her daughter,
making sure she notices the delicacy

with which the man controls the tweezers, revolves
the moth's abdomen through the florescence
                    until it is only the artifice of moth—

                        a mirage which, if ever obtained,
(if the lamp is carried far enough, the bird sighted high enough,
the dress found in water)
                        destroys the image.

Seventeen, I remember her age, your sister,
an Easter Sunday when we hit the market

& the burning started. Navy men, stationed
near Pend Oreille, peacocked their suits

around the square.
                    When she stirred

through the fruit stands, holding a plum so ripe
its peeling bruised, the men pivoted in the ache

with which a migrating songbird,
distracted by phosphor,
                 forgets the route roted by constellations
in the phosphorus of its feathers.

        Alas. We are tired of stars
        & stroll under the skyline's
        electric wash. When you draw close
        I feel phosphorus & not phosphor.
        When you wander near the ornaments
        of shop lights, your frame etches
        against the window the way rain breaks
        silver on sidewalks. From somewhere:
        the drum of tires on streets,
        the hum of bug wings on air,
        the hum of street lamps whitening on wind.
        We leave that section & stop & sit
        on a bench. The sky is a marble
        dropped in water. A disoriented swallow
        flies around a lighted window, exhausted.

On a plum branch, she hung one of the empty
coke bottles she'd lured
into a birdfeeder, the red water a filler for warmth

a hungry hummingbird takes, heart hard-pressed
to wing beats, feathers patched with enough adrenaline
to trick the sun. We are so overwhelmed with emotion

we move both backwards & forwards at once.
Though some emit a heartlight violet enough

to consume them. A match struck
in the lowest oxygen chamber of her lungs.

A lantern rose along & keenly lit her face,
her eyes the skyline
birdmen exhausted over in their polished shoes.

Floret as Bird

1.

What is hunger if I once listened to a floret
slurp storm water into soil, sex a spore on wind,

a single seed left for a bird to eat.
I could not call you, would not

call you anything other than—Like, say, in the shallows
of the river we laid crawdad traps until our fingers pruned.

Oxblood-colored bank: where we uprooted
clay, molded wet grains into plates, set them on some
stones to harden. Shoes soaked in silt, we swelled,

a hunger heavy as a field of florets, feathers
dreamed sprouting from skin. Hunger of when one is

lost once in another. I touched your eyelid,
watched you shutter. Anything other than—

Returning to the room, I wrenched the radio high
enough to string static over traffic, trees & shore.
When the speakers slipped white sparrow bones

to the ceiling, I graced your palm,
guided us under the fan's hot breath,

held you close enough to consume
your sweat. We swayed our limbs, moving them
through momentary doors. A hibiscus hid

in light. Every second: no surface held
the same pigments exactly—how a bird
must feel a hundred feet from earth.

Radio off: rupturing
the room in robin plumes of silence. We devoured
crawdads off mud plates, fracturing
shells between our flesh,

juice dripping from fingers
made to bear the weight of being
wingless.

2.

I postured at the window—
the ridge like earth's raised shoulderblade,

the mountain line laying out weary as an arm.
Water slumped in my squat glass.

> We walk into a slapload
> of sunlight & say goodbye. As you
> turn towards your car, I remain
> holding your hand: arms
> the beam
> from a flashlight, bodies
> the brilliance it burns towards &
> the bulb it propels from—though
> the light between
> is a mere flicker of dimmed dust & air.

What is restlessness if I wake up
with a peacock's plume

inside my thighs?
Past the frame, a cardinal, red cowl

> I'll be fine. I'll be
>   fine. I'll be

on its neck, folded
the air to origami. Months later I routed

>   A sensation navigated,
>   a traveled way,
>   the line from which an end emerges.

our migration on a map.
The journey scaled the thickness of a quill.

>   I could not
>   continue. Calling you
>   bird.
>   & you made
>   me   pay for   this.

With the cardinal lost to horizon,
you routed

                    A sense of wild
confusion,   to rummage,   to not continue
calling you   bird   & to pay for this.

your hand on my shoulder, told me our lungs
were sewn together, but with a loosening stitch,

        Disrupted by ourselves
        we do not notice each
        others' overwhelming appetites.

so when one of us talks, the other
must fill our shared chest with breath,

        So
        dependant &
        this sickens us.
        What is a person
        other than the way
        we root, like a cicada, that plated bird,
        into the other's consciousness, only to
        rebirth, once every seventeen years, when the earth is
        torn up—

        The cicadas are spawning, & the birds,
        the birds are,

must flap until the wind recedes,
must guard our nest over each other's wandering eyes.
(Over a bird too ornamental for the realities of gravity).

        Bird,   know
        the birds are   feasting.

3.

You spoke:

> The shallows are murky
> where your feet floundered.

your spine a river
& my chest a cutbank.

> Drawing your hands
> from the current, you drape water
> down your hair so strands

Your ribs stone pillars
& my mouth constant wind.

> settle on your neck. As you turn
> to me, a thread dissects
> your forehead. Skitter bugs

My hand a shovel
& your stomach hard earth.

> crackle over the sound
> of river falling from you.
> You smell the way people ought to:

Loving someone, you said, is knowing
how you are a destruction of their life.

> torn from skin towards the current
> of song, wind, & root.

4.

Rain wrung out, a dirty
dishrag. Sunlight
igniting the dandelions.

On a poplar limb, a crow drapes
wet wings. From its tail, a drop pinned

into a puddle
where an ant circles, centers

upside down & sinks. I am certain
only in the instability of matters as the tailpipe

of my Buick leaves a feather of smoke,
silken for a moment, before the smoke

extincts to sky, the sky
the crow crosses through.

5.

When winter renames the windrows in snow,
she downs in the plumage of blankets,

the warmer perch of furnace.
Hawking her eyes
to the window, she watches a V of geese

confide southward in wind, wings steering & shifting
the friction. Together they hit the horizon's height:

        Bird,   know

from which shift of wind
                hunger emerges.

6.

We lay in a nest of covers. Lamplight drew
in the cleave of your breasts
florets of yellow. Breathing,

bright to shadow, egg-white to pains-grey.
(red riverbank, speak of crawdads
          red riverbank, speak of shore fires)

    Kneeling near the river I reach in
    both palms, pull them up, as if to soothe
    my face, though I only hold
    them out, watching water materialize.

Leaning over me, you drew lips

    A glop of clay rests between my fingers.
    I pass it to you & you set it in a basket.
    Basket full, we sit on a large stone.
    The sky is a well where the water is
    too far down to see. We set the plates
    on a slab of earth & stand there,
    in the night, with no one
    but the thrumming of the current.
    Highway lights muted through trees.

above my adams apple, lines feathered

from your eyes. I could call you
another. Anything other than—

Two cardinals, in the garden,
ruffled their wings against each other,

one bird rising, the other knocking it down.
Your arms loomed over

my throat, pupils the brown spots
on robin eggs. *Tell me we will never be*
those birds.

Moisture in the Lungs

Winter—Rain reveals in layers
what lumps rose the snowline.
Bodies buried beneath white wreckage.

Winter—Moisture presses its blue belly to the sky.
A coming storm goosebumps the air.

Winter—The ground smells like light lost
in a well's bottom. The night before the rain,

I asked if we would ever fit
into each other's bathrobes. The space between:

a paper lantern, luminous
from a distance, but too fragile for anything more

than the tenderness of a finger. Winter—When yours
traced my throat, the way you'd test a plum

for ripeness, we were lying on a blanket,
on the floor, & I said *tomorrow*

maybe we should drive into Montana, make a day of it,
stop off at an interstate buffet & eat some
figs. There was a pause where I could hear
the overhead fan stir dust around its light.

Winter—I woke to long arms of air, hairs
standing on end against the sky. The sun, rising,
was caught smoldering through the grey,

& had relented, & turned
back. My skin felt like I hadn't drunk water
in three days. Winter—I admit an emptiness

I make in mistaking difficult
for intolerable. Who am I other than a stain
on those who have dry-cleaned my suits,
eaten stews beside me under lamplight,
shared the same water browned from pipe rust?

Winter—You trailed me, though I wasn't
going anywhere. Silver stitches of rain battered
the air. As I turned around, hoping, like snow
melting down a hillside, to see what foliage

had survived, I saw you, in your scarf.
Sloshy flakes clung to your clothes & hair.
Your eyes, brown behind your breath—
a window mirroring the motion

of a man throwing a rock right at its glass.
Over the hills clouds formed in one long grey finger,
reached out, seeped into my lungs, & stirred.

On Air & Angels: The Numbers

A young John Donne, just some boy before he entered the clergy, stepped from his office into the hallway. His skull felt stuffed with sound, his heart with crumpled-up pieces of blank paper. Though, the pains he felt from sitting for four fruitless hours at his desk couldn't compare to the pains caused by his wife's father. Only poets are naive enough to believe they can manipulate numbers in their own way—that two could become one when one of those is such a larger number. & so the page, or what small self-loathing inked the page, read *John Donne, Ann Donne, un-done.* He looked back at his study. On the desk, a column of light, yes, some celestial energy, an angel maybe, carrying indefinite specks of dust, their bodies luminous, materials made possible by something traveling here from the heavens. The numbers endlessly in front of him.

Table 2.1

Gas	Activities Causing Emissions	Affected Area
Carbon Dioxide (CO2)	primarily fossil fuel burning, secondarily deforestation	My father has worked on a logging outfit for a little over a decade. When he was in his twenties, though, he foremaned on a hot shot crew called The Helen of Troys, which navigated the burned up bottoms of forests around the Pacific Northwest, hacking through old growth, lighting backfires in huckleberry brush. Now, when the sun goes down, late in the evening, sky fumes around his house & he begins to sweat, reaching to where a hatchet used to hang on his overalls. Every day he drives a Backhoe through a section of land clear of trees so that the remaining stumps look like the stubble on a man's face. He drinks RC Cola in the heat & thinks it's unusual he used to ache up a mountain after an aspen grove, & now can barely stand to sit on a felled sequoia at lunch. His new crew, he knows, will shortly turn his seat into a two by four. Some people chase a fire long enough the heat consumes them.
Chlorofluorocarbons (CFCs)	refrigerators, foam insulation & packing, previously spray cans— now banned	Wearing a fishing cap with a treble hook snared in its mesh, my little brother, Marcellus, sprays a ladybug with a can of Lysol. In a puddle of chemicals the bug writhes. Marcellus flags over the insect, leaning back & forth so his shadow swallows & regurgitates it. Across the yard my father is dumping a busted refrigerator into the back of Jerry's truck. Jerry is my father's younger brother. A few nights ago Jerry climbed into Marcellus's window. It was three a.m. & he was drunk & had mistaken the window for that of my mother's office. When Marcellus opened his eyes, he smelled perspiration like Lysol, & he saw Jerry's face, strained & pale, his belly smeared against the sill. Jerry flicked his

arms & legs, struggling to gain ground. Marcellus drops the spray can. Be quiet, Marcellus says, leaning his lips near the ladybug, You don't want to wake your father.

Methane (CH4)	rice paddies, ruminant animals, coal mining, natural gas leaks, landfills

Standing at the kitchen window, Jerry seams apart curtains made from an old tablecloth. He holds a bologna & mayo sandwich. He hasn't taken a bite, but is instead panning across the field at the landfill. Sunlight fumigates over steel cars, refrigerators, & empty spray cans. Above the piles, clouds clot, a greenish-grey. When Jerry was a young GI stationed near Hanoi, he stalked along a marsh, beside rice paddies, & smelled the aroma of a trash bag's plastic lining. From the rice stalks, a Vietcong sprouted, arms raised. In his hand a silver sickle mirrored the foliage. If Jerry hadn't stopped to sniff whatever chemical fled over the water, the blade would have plucked his temple, but instead hit the sergeant walking beside him. Jerry curtained the sergeant in his arms & blood oiled in the man's stubble. In the field across from Jerry's kitchen window, a cow chews regurgitated grass. Jerry thinks cows are disgusting creatures & he can remember (a few months after he was shipped home) working as a coal miner in Beulah when an angus wandered into the road. In North Dakota, roads can lead everywhere & nowhere & in some places you are lucky to see a house every fifteen miles. When he hit the cow, his foreman was riding shotgun. The cow was kept by the man who outfitted their mining operation, & both Jerry & the foreman knew, if reported, the worth of beef would be taken from their pay. Tired from working the brunt end of a seven on stretch, they loaded the steer, heavy as several refrigerators, into the truck bed & drove into the mountains. They delivered the animal into an abandoned shaft, listening to wind friction over the cow's body, the wind like the whistle of a coal worker who's happy he's not starving.

Nitrus oxide (N2O)	nitrogenous fertilizers, burning fossil fuels & biomass	

Jerry sits on my father's tractor, eating the lunch my mother made, looking out over the land my grandfather allotted to the oldest son. Past the sweet potato rows, mountains rototill blue sky. Above their ridges, a cowtail of clouds stretch. For the last three hours Jerry spread fertilizer, his shirt browned from sweat. When he bites the sandwich, he tastes exhaust & he turns off the ignition & waits for the fumes to clear. While a GI, he once stepped into a village & was suddenly hit with a white phosphorus bomb. For a moment, the smoke was so thick he could feel it in his ears. In the field that morning, the tractor kicked up enough dirt that he had to wrap a handkerchief around his mouth. When he stopped the tractor his tongue was still coated in dust. Taking a bite of his sandwich, he tastes dirt & processed pork, & remembers in Hanoi how the smoke cleared, & he heard an explosion: the collapse of huts, water troughs tipping over, oxen & roosters scurrying into brush, men exposing noise from their throats. A fertilizer bomb turns a moment into corpses. Those too severed to be sent home were planted into the Hanoi soil. Often now, Jerry dreams that his friends shoot up, half human, half plant material, & live among the villagers, eating stones & straw, drinking pond water beside oxen. They are waiting out humanity's extinction. Jerry starts the tractor & its engine shutters. A platoon of birds, so large they cover the canopy, lift from the field & demand the sky.

A Footprint in the Snow. The Snow Fills It in.

In the forest, in the snow, five miles past my house
I found a fieldguide. Not as damaged as you would
think, the pages, grey with hail, still held, ink blurred
at the edges, as if the shape and meaning remained
out of focus. As if winter planned to write
not love notes, but of how the bird's brown bruises
on sky scarred its margins in shadow. This winter
was the last spent wondering why your eyes

are different shades. The bird seemed to understand,
& kept its distance, weary, the field its guide
to how large a shadow can loom. Bird, a clump of rat bones
lodged in my throat. I went inside, set the fieldguide down
where it situated sunlight around its dust. There is no end
to light & shadow, only ourselves doubled over
& over through a field, guided by how skin scatters

vapors. And there is no end to you & I, only the way
we spend every day pretending to forget.
Then why does it feel like someone has
scrawled chalk in my lungs? Before you left, I pretended we
still held close to the hallelujah of our sweat. We could still
cross the field without giving away whether one, or no,
or two people had been strong enough, or restrained enough,
to tread across the field without leaving any markings.

Fieldguide to the Southeastern Idaho Phosphate District

[An Introduction to the Cycle]

The southeastern corner of Idaho, just east of Soda Springs—a woman reminded me of someone I met, once, in the woodsmoke of the patio on my uncle's property, the last summer before he went to prison. Things turn sometimes & you end up in a place you surely thought someone would be, just not yourself. Or that person is you, though you are no longer who you'd trained yourself to live with, & hardly recognize the expressions in the mirror. The way her gaze, your gaze, (I admit, it was always you) attenuated outwards towards the junipers, though I could tell, as you fringed the hem of your sundress, that you were inside yourself, investigating, running over & over, like a waterwheel, like infinity, like time, whatever it was that nourished you. A feeding. We do this to ourselves, this erudition. Years later, calmly whispering into the receiver became the same as shouting at you, heart full of woodsmoke, across that field. It was a sort of loss, as if I were only remembering a conversation we'd had, & needed to search it out, as you'd searched out whatever it was you had to find before it—bright as decay, a reckoning—found you.

[Structural Setting of Bird & Phosphor]

Most fieldguides illustrate the events influencing a landscape. But how can we relay what needs said without sounding like we've scavenged the husk of a road-side whitetail. Do you believe, as Freud did, that we are self-destructive? Acid-lined & rooted, deeply, beneath what we consciously perceive? To frame it this way the senses are an illusion. ∴ We want to fuck our mothers not because they are so, but because sex is a sort of death, & how dare they create & get away with it? Or, like Skinner, do we only seek whatever gives us pleasure, a species of hedonists? ∴ No morals other than dopamine. Aren't they the same? ∴ The times you begged me (& it was a begging) to pin your wrists to the mattress, to overrule your breath with the sound of gravel. I am not who you think I am & so I hurt you. You are not who I think you are & so you hurt me. ∴ Like a dog salivating at the sound of a bell, I realized that when you bruised my most tender of organs, you saw me, hairy chest & stench of dick, as I saw myself, & I was happy. ∴ We called this a History of Intimacy, & thought about it as we drove by the phosphate mines. Men emerged from earth, wheezing because the air was too bright. They were not used to being treated this way & drove home to their families who glowed so white that the men had to shield their eyes—sons with clean fingernails, daughters tragic enough to date boys who wanted to be miners, wives who hated hearing canaries sing because it sounded too much like their own names.

[A Brief History of Urine]

Not yet knowing that phosphate is an essential component of DNA, Hennig Brand, hunched into a ratty robe like a fat scarecrow, held a vial of elemental phosphorus, which he'd extracted from the four-glasses-of-wine-worth of his own urine. The things we wash ourselves of are vital to our survival. Again, I have woken in a whiskey sweat next to you, separating the chemicals of breath. What is it you ask me. I say when I am comfortable. The answer will be different from the moths, those half-birds, believing the light wants to be smudged by their love. Around us, like ashes from a forest fire, they are falling.

Bladders burning
of vodka

& Gatorade, we
drive a part of road
that one hour
later would be

closed. Horizon light a dirty
fingerprint & we

shutter the Buick's axle

over weeds. Not
from the bottom where it grounds,
but from the top,

where it gives, a billboard

brightens with smoke.
An image

of a dairy
cow—ashing into the already

dirty air. See, you say, nothing
holds how

it should.

[Sieving]

You, a
woman who
cannot, call
me when
I am

getting into
bed. You are
about to

fail at something
important, not
because you
can't but because

you don't
think very much
of how

your hair falls &
see how hard it
is to say
this. The
moment I
try to air

fills my
mouth & somewhere,
possibly beneath
the mine
slag in
your lungs, you

know
this is true, &
I'm just
being
honest. If you
make me

feel terrible I
might feel
about you the way
you feel about white

girls walking
out of
a smoothie &

tan shop. That
is, you are
free to

be loose. We talk
about it one
night when the road
is closed off. No

returning where we need
to. No sound
anywhere but for

both of us this
is the
better part,
the way we love

each others'
gaps.

[Dry Valley Mine]

1.

The air—
sandpaper,
walking through
a cornfield
in late Autumn.

2.

Hair uncombed, lips blue with sleep, you smeared the suds from my fingers on your dress & went to bed. Night, all of it, I heard you scuttling, trying to find sheets that didn't feel like a moth in the gut. I got up & turned on the lamp, its light gulping the room. When I couldn't stand the way you looked in it, I walked outside. At the fence, a caribou, fur scraggy, ribs pressing on skin like a man trying to force his hands through. The caribou must have wanted something to hold off its hunger for sleep. Approaching it, I displayed my empty palms. I offered it what I offer you.

[So Just Migrate]

Somewhere in the Selkirk Mountains, my uncle stepped off his snowmobile, took a sip of the coffee he brought with him in a thermos. He was a man who believed in bigfoot, & the snow was falling hard around him. His breath rose through the scarf snugged to his mouth, the fabric wet from breath. When he turned towards his vehicle, he saw, in the snow, a footprint larger than his boots. A few seconds & snow filled it in. This was the story he told me when I told him that the last herd of caribou left in the lower forty-eight had abandoned that range of mountains. They were tired of eating lichen, hearing the loud noises of engines, knowing that cougars found it easier to stalk the packed tracks of a snowmobile. Everything moves on, eventually, he said, & looked at me—a man who had come to get drunk with him because my girlfriend had left me for the second of several times. Sometimes, what you need & what you feed on aren't in the same area, he said.

[Enoch Valley Mine]

There are
times when
you
are heavier
with booze. Breath
a weight
of its own
opening, how
I never taste
the inner
ridge where
minerals
are, how I
excavate
too harshly &
without
the proper
tools. Even when
I finally
have what I've
been secluding
myself from
the sun for, I
don't know how
to handle it,
the weight
too dissimilar
to my own. I
want to unearth
you
in an
orange
dress sewn for
the plateaus. Like
a hunk of
sky chunked through
a mineshaft's
surface
vent, you blare too
much of the nutrients
I've been
starving of.

[Driving past the slag piles, covered in pollen. Shadows of clouds spotting the mounds]

If ever entered   a mine shaft must be seen out to its conclusion   the light
at its end expected   a sort of relief   not that it's there   but that we might
start dealing with it ∴ Last Wednesday   we invited over for a barbecue the
only three friends of mine you could utter a syllable towards ∴ In the mid-
dle of folding onions into meat   you   or maybe it *was* me   said something
only meant to be tested inside the beetle-&-bat-burrows of the brain Gritty
as they are   Everything spoils once confronted with air   It was not fin-
ished when the first guests arrived ∴ *Hello how are you   We're fine thanks
The burgers are already on   Step outside in the shade*   She placed my cloth
sack   two books   & a toothbrush   by the door ∴ A symbol   By the door
∴ Even before that   a year before   I was at the grocery store   near the
register   eating some M&M's   Late at night   A woman clearly furious
walked in with her husband   Bless her   someone   bless her   She refused
to hide her rage   Not uttering a word   she bought a small sack of smoked
almonds with food stamps   Her husband hustled behind her   desperate
looking   dandruff on his shoulders   wearing a Hamburgler shirt   He
wheelbarrowed his worries on me   *You know   kings never used to live like
me   I live better than kings did centuries ago*   His wife frictioned her shoes
on the tile   refusing to look at him   *Not even Kings had the things I have*
the vibration of his voice   more honest than I'd ever be   was directed
at the reaction on my face   one his wife might catch ∴ She cracked an
almond in her jaw   Or the day before our guests arrived   when you told
me something you felt necessary   and in the middle of your speech   I
said   *yes   yes   I understand*   though I still had to sit &   listen to an
end   you couldn't stop chasing.

[Simplot Smoky Canyon Mine]

Sitting beside me so I would shield the smoke you threw out or more accurately   you
tested out its weight in the air the buoyancy of it in the smoke a thing between us

which   hovering

no possible relief

tom squatting on

it a sort of trick

cents   swathed

Around us the

mutated some-

displayed in fast

sprouting sped

looks choppy &

I say it? Did we

er?) are they too

With so many

c   o   m   e

[Between us]

a bowl of soup
cools, a sprig of cilantro,

muddied from steam &
similar
to an insect skimming

the secret tension of
water, floats
in the middle, & neither

of us wants to
confess into the herb's

delicate balance, neither
of us wants to
overturn it.

would either dissipate or be suspended
You held a glass by its bottom the bot-
your palm as if you were balancing
The alcohol near red under floures-
teetered back & forth as we talked
bar its crowd piano notes & lights
thing like a nature documentary
forward the long process of a plant
up so that what is most natural
artificial Our lives you asked (or did
only acknowledge it silently togeth-
much this way? This stuttering?
time lapses how could we possibly
to   terms   with   one   another?

On Air & Angels: The Reconciliation of Twos

With the sound of a clapping, no, more than a sound, a sensation of the sound in his brain, Donne woke. The air smelled of leaf-smoke drifting through rain. Silence candlelit the room. Donne kicked his sheets aside & walked to his desk where one wick burned low. From the bed, Anna mumbled, some dream stumbling from her lips. But did he see *her* at first? The mole on her back, a bloated cross. Where her spine knotted, the water-worn pages of a book, the bible maybe. No. First he thought not of her, but of who she was as an idea—born to someone higher than himself, the daughter of a politician. No matter what he wrote on god, one plus one would never equal, as he wanted it to, one. Metaphysicians, like himself, believed not in twos, as he was confronted with, but threes. Some celestial, aerial, & material. Some god, angel, & us others. Some infinite, some temporary, & the angels, thank goodness, in between. Those gracious things. A reconciliation. *If only, Anna, I could find a way.* She turned so that the flesh of her shoulders shone, her neck where the hair allowed halos of skin. What could he get from this body other than what he'd already had? Though what more did he want than to hunger for it as her skin wrinkled, as flesh gave over to shadows, his cravings a generation seeding itself repeatedly through muscle & bone?

On Uprooting

The oaks are bare of any honest
testament of leaves. The sky a slight prayer

of snowfall. & you, of winter rains,
fog scribbled over on the car's window.

    Mosquitoes sirened
    to a discharge
    of light we
    know
    nothing better
    than what comes
    to us
    distorted.

Materializing through the grey bloom,
you are dressed appropriate for florets—
your dandelion coat, your scarf,

pearls of rain streaming on sunflower petals.
(Think not of oak trees, but leaves,

not of grey bugs on streetlamps,
but the shadows moths flutter around roads).

    The hours white
    with rain, you
    step close. In my
    chest, a flame
    narrows
    to the proportions
    of a feather. Lips
    perched, you suspend
    me in the weight
    of lungs.
    The flame could
    either give
    over
    or grow.

A bird gongs on the after-autumn air.

A rain-gouged field—
a small cardinal, wings torn,
feathers splayed
to frilled string.
When our shadows
overrule it, it struggles
to breathe, scraping
along the ground. I draw
my pocketknife. You pretend
the blade is too bright.
Sometimes you have to
ruin something to save it.

We bring this to the lake:
vodka, a basket brimmed with apples.
A cocktail of get up, let down.

Before us: a wasteland
of birches—ruins resilient

in the fog. Pumpkins whitening
around black mold. Leaves stenching the rain-
gutters: the feelings of another.

I stand at the full-length mirror.
My eyes blasted white, shoulders pale,
penis tipped to one side. When you emerge,
you thread your fingers through my rib-ruts,
say feathers fray
the wind, shift
the wind-shifts
the wind.

The foliage of sky flushes to plum. I carry on like a lantern

& promise we'll return when the weather
allows room for ripples, for failures, & amends, amen.

When the woods open to salt lamps,
dusk reveals the tunnel ends of train light the sky keeps.

Uproots the sky—
Run beside its whitest horizon.

As we cross into the city, I cherish the empty:
shoveling into snow until fingers lose feeling
& lungs light cold as apple cores & you realize

you were always meant for a meaningless uprooting—
that below the snow is dead grass, & below the grass
are dead roots, & below the roots a trail of water
runs always away from you. On the other side

of a kitchen window, a woman raises a glass,
carefully drinking, the light, behind her, her only hallelujah—

Summer has long rendered its light to the eclipse of geese.
Autumn pressing a grey lid over the land. But before this:

Following the compass of palm lines on wind, I journeyed
to the lake. The bank hadn't already given its flesh

over to ice. I knelt & watched an insect angel wings
above a shallow. A trout triggered in the air & both disappeared.

From their wake, one ripple merged into another,
blunt end to blunt end, together confronting the bank.

A single flake fell into the shallow, absolving

hardened mass to warmth. I needed to hear your name,
not bird, distorted over the surface, shattered in reeds

& reassembled—
the magnet made from our bodies,
how water catalogues its dependence on other water.

Newton & the Law of Celeste's Body

Picture Newton walking towards the field's edge with a shovel & no shirt. His work on the irrigation ditch was finished, so he waited on a mound of knapweed, gently scraping the shovel's end against grass. After an hour, Celeste, the daughter of his father's friend, motioned towards him, carrying a glass of water. She handed him the glass, squinting into the trench. She said it appeared his work was finished. "Yesterday," Newton said, "I saw a girl eating at those graves." He pointed to the graves right before the road. A side of Celeste's cheek caved in where she was biting her flesh. "All the time," she said, "girls come around." Sunlight shone on the drape below her neck. "A day this nice would force a body outside." But Newton was still looking towards the road. Again, a week later, Newton stood at the graves, hoping the girl would curve the bend. After he stared at dirt for a few moments, Celeste emerged, handing him another glass of water. "The mechanics of it," Newton said, gesturing towards the bend, "should be rational. She should be here today, if she was before." Tired of weak force, Celeste grabbed Newton's hand & orbited it on her, gravitating towards his ear. "Attraction," she said, "is controlled by the strength of a body & its proximity to another. If a girl is closer," her voice cosmic in his canal, "her force is stronger."

The Aether Notes

A dark rut the river is beyond

where a dragonfly turquoises the grass,
here, & a plane creates its own cloud, there.

Despite this space, I know—
The rain among many voices.
Scrubgrass for gestures of wind.

Stones for water vapored to grey air.
I know. I know. The Electroweak squelching smoke

    The Electro-
    weak
    walks into
    the bar. She satellites
    the phone to her
    ear. The overhead
    florescent heliums
    on her bracelet.

from her hair in the hotel shower.
Or the Strong shaking dried sunflower leaves
(dried in the sun)
from his shoes. I know

disassembling, of
unmappable space.

               *

I arrive at the river—
water is slower & cooler,
rain is a periphery, &
I am
thinking of Mankato, Minnesota,
the jukebox a siren
no one could serenade to. *Do me wrong. Do me right.*
Do me like you knew you always would.

    The Strong, sitting at the bar
    long enough to crumple

three napkins, slouches into a beer,
the horizon of his spine dawning,
the vacuous below his legs
a blackhole. The visions go
on   like this. I know another
(   ) man orbits him.
The music of the room fills his cup.

*

Shadows—If
this man resembled the ashen
stains under my eyes. A birthmark,
on my neck, shaped like the inlet of a river.

    You drift a finger
    over the birthmark, as if
    its current
    could take you
    to the wider body
    of my body.
    It will. We
    drown in our own
    flesh.
    We, bloated & barely
    breathing, begin to
    surface here.

*

Between then & now
is traced, like a body of water
contained in earth, by transition:

never always there, or here, never an ending
or a beginning, but rather an infinite, flowing

present. The movement through history
a movement through space.

The straight line of centuries replaced
by a body drifting forwards, backwards,

left & right; a body of history
moving beyond the dimensions .

so that every movement & moment is part
past & future. The moment, if it exists at all—

One ripple breaking & another
preparing to be pushed forth.

*

In an attic overlooking the street
I sift through several pages of notes:

*The electroweak is a combination of two
of the fundamental interactions of nature.
Electromagnetism, which is responsible
for all the bonds of daily life, & the weak,
which is responsible for decay.*

*The strong is a force that lures particles
through a positive charge. Surprisingly
these are all different aspects
of the same phenomenon—love.*

*

So then how does one say I was here, on this day,
in this bar, watching my girlfriend the Electroweak
speak to some man the Strong? How do I locate
myself while simultaneously accounting
for the losses endured to both before & after I,
not the dragonfly but its shed skin,

I breathe over you,
still pressed inside,
your hands clasping the muscles
we follow,
a rhythm of
the other's inhales—
no new hydrogen or oxygen
entering the air. So many
metamorphoses
are the same
as before. Restlessness, &
I am looking for my own
reflection
in this aether
but only seeing

another
muddle of
sweat between
our stomachs,
a static shock.
Sweat between your breasts:
broken glass & us
broken.

met her at the river?
Somewhere on the scale

    I sacrifice my hands
    under the bathroom sink.
    I am so busy admiring
    the mirror I don't notice
    the water is not on.

from lantern shine to shade.
The white edge of an eye

    Arched into
    the door,
    you are a flushed
    husk where
    in the mirror we
    meet & know it is
    over, though
    neither of us
    says so.

to the white rim of a streetlamp.

    The drapes are pregnant
    with traffic lights. We
    never should have stayed
    in a hotel in a town
    named after a misspelled
    tribal word.
    Blue earth. I sit at the end
    of the bed, buckle into
    another smoke, & as I light it
    I brace my hands
    around the flame, hoping you will
    not receive any of its light. Lying there, staring
    into no known heaven, you won't
    speak for hours.

*

(pastpastpresentpresentpastpresentpast-
past   presentpastpastpastpresent   pastpastpresentpastpast
)

*

See your shadow,
blipped on a larger

surface, moving over its surface,
before you pass

> The riverbank—
> Why do we
> return to flares.
> The water murmurs
> a bat into reeds.
> I taste the river—gnats
> near the shallows, cattails,
> the film of dead fish
> banked on stones.

into a space beyond
the rain-rotted paper of one human to another.

*

If there is a minimum distance—
one moment to another—

there would have to be
some sort of shift. Though

an aether is endlessly between flares
of energy, & to notice it, to step inside

its white-grey & recognize anything
resembling yourself,
is where you could say, finally,

I was here, or there, on this day, or another,
if for a moment. My own myself.

Star & gaslight are traveling
on a vacuum of wind & river-reeds.

A sunflower arches its head into the sun.
When the shade lengthens,
it returns its attention to the house again.

So that if you were there, on any given day,
at the same time as another, you
could not remember, later,
which day was before, or after.

*

Clearly time is told in time,
contains both itself & the one who tells it.
There is so little room there for sunflowers,

for the horizon
where hand & hand almost touch,
where the lantern's & the water's edge meet,

where river-sand scrapes lungs,
where spine, wrist, & shin circuit
a weak charge from one callused heart valve to another.

*

Sky a body, which water capes: moon-white & endlessly
in front of us. On the bank the lantern's flame
has bent low so that the land behind us
is empty of form. Shall we step forward or fall back?
I know the water by the way it charges a vein.
Shall we give over our energy, restlessly, to this aether?
I know the owls by the way their wings block stars.
Shall we wade, hands brushing but not held, into the water
&, seeing ourselves doubled on its surface,
admit that we have been here before
& are now witnessing ourselves returning, together,
as young & handsome as we are today?
I know the surface by what it confronts in myself.

    Static.
    Like soot

on an ashtray,
light smudges
the counter. Music, muscle,
the man's breath.

*

We begin to curve that spacetime: in the barroom
where music seeps into the vaulted ceiling.

In the river water which flows white & endlessly
into the sky we step towards.

On the bank where a dragonfly lanterns on a dead lamp.
In the hotel room where the door opens.

    (Here, now, quick, now)

A man stands in its frame. Scraps of dried sunflower
at his feet. Across the road a neon sign mimics
a star before the door closes.

*

    From the trees behind me I hear
a shaking & turn
& watch a lantern, only a lantern,
    the light materializing the brush,
until the woman who carries it nears enough—
    yours eyes &
    the light
at last.

Experiments in the Field of Light

[Patterns of Light Migration]

Sketches of morning: a streetlamp hums bugs. When the heat collapses, the bugs scatter. Sun on sky, sun on grass, sun on rooftops, ponds, & pavement. I press my palm to the lawn where the blades imprint this atmosphere—Of moth wings. Of streetlamps. Of hallelujah.

The background noise
is visible. Wind through willow limbs

the rustle of pages flipped through.
The radio static of insects clattering

around a streetlamp. When I
speak into the shed where you are

splitting wood, I watch my words
rise white mist. Behind me, the door

thuds shut & you
startle into where sunlight makes
the sawdust suspend.

[Objectives of Location]

It is August & wind tumbleweeds
through the grass. The field is bright as a sheet of ice.

Shadows of a willow string my skin.
This morning, resting your head
on my lap, your hair draped my legs.

As I stranded
my fingers through, I listened
to the ceiling fan mimic weather.

No longer chopping
the light, the fan clattered
still, & our eyes opened
a closed space infinitely.

[Multiplicities of One]

Always be breathing in the light of another. Use it up.
I aim a flashlight

at the constellations & wonder
where their words
will meet.

The word for bug & dust. Barn &
cat. For star, stone,
& ultraviolet. Ultimately, for man

& woman.

As we lie in bed, I speak softly into the lamp bleaching
your eyelids. A song

of unending resurrections.

[Song Unending]

Moonlight opens on floral sheets where your body should be. Smells of wet wood, sleep sweat, the dust of curtains. I step onto the porch where it is midnight or sometime after. Sky mildews, skin is sticky & cooling. Something I cannot see, maybe you, is making noises, a scrapping sound, a rummage. I point the flashlight into the fog. Its light births successively on every molecule until, in a flutter, your silhouette—a woman pretty enough to make the birds shut up—flickers towards me. Every moment is, light particle by light particle, reborn.

[Participants of Light & Shadow]

I listen as you exhale into the whine of the ceiling fan. Around us the house is dark & slow. I rise, air snaps my skin. A tire fire controls the horizon—colored as tin sheeting left to rust in rainlight. I feel another man orbiting me, a flickering, white phosphor of a man. A projection of myself, strained & semi-transparent. I watch the man sit up in bed. He leans over where your face is exposed to the ceiling. He draws the covers back over your shoulders. You startle & breathe into the dustlamp. When you turn over, the man rises & walks towards me. I feel a steel ball of light thud on my lungs. We step to the sill & look out to where the tire fire has begun to smolder. Orion scratches, stuttering out of view. As I return to bed, the man wavers in & out of me. A whirl of dust connects with a wooden blade above us.

[Light Withdrawals]

Because my side of the sheet has lost light's warmth, I scoot close, press my stomach to your spine. We share what makes us visible.

[Transmigration]

White moths furrow in wind, a reflection of them, patterned, shifting—a plume of sawdust. Another hundred generations & the smoke will grey them. In their shadow we share a glass of water. We get up. We, hand and hand with wandering steps, and slow. A hologram: our bodies on the shifting pigments. Through light we took this solitary way.

Array

For light to hold, or after. For light—silhouettes of striking—to clasp on
to us, hulls who can't carry it. Or after. What dust does when the curtains close.

Let's renew ourselves there, that paper season of behavior, you & me husked
to one another, particles of what the day likes to combust, you & me beaming
        under affairs

of damage. DNA, disturbed in a sun splotch, carry forward, if you would,

the bright wreckage of us. The street, papered in yesterday's parade
of blossoms, rouses you, sleep-deprived but battered by morning,
                                                to the pavement-wet wrap
of humidity, the porchlamp left on. How many of us are
                                useless by noon? Pupils
narrowing, you turn to me & speak—No.
Let's renew ourselves where our bodies eclipsed last night's moon-less emissions,
        a sort of ring

of time never met by light, so that at that hour,
                any hour of dark, we appeared
different. Not a shadow but what a shadow swallows.

II

Why else, but at this moment of blindness,
would I mold the contours of my sweat to yours? If a bat, wings

What Does the World Consist Of?

of stretched, veiny flesh, were to ruck-up
what tiny particles of appearance somehow endured the day,

it could not even perceive with those burrow-born eyes that separate
heat-sources disrupted

its sonar. Isn't that what love is? Us hungering
        for an indistinguishable presence
in a world we will never navigate? Or is it,

while still in the bat's ricocheted mapping
        of half a half-light, to suddenly
separate from who we drew
our warmth for—animals confronting our own

sensory competence? Whether we even believe the sun is eight light-minutes from
        earth.

MICROSCOPIC AND MACROSCOPIC PHENOMENA
Natural science today is mainly concerned with two areas of
investigation: the macroscopic (ultimately represented by astro-
phenomena) and the microscopic (ultimately repre-
sented by the elementary particles of nature); see Figure 1.
Since the study of cosmological problems is our objective, we
begin by reviewing in this chapter that part of our astronomical
knowledge which is relevant for this purpose. However, the
microscopic world, provides indispensable terms of reference for
understanding the macroscopic in the next chapter we
pertinent aspects of particle physics. Furthermore
the behavior of a collection of particles under conditions ofte
found in the cosmic environment is of major importance i
understanding astrophysical and cosmological phenomena, so i
Chapter IV we review the appropriate aspects of plasma physic

SOLAR SYSTEMS AND GALAXIES

Let us begin with a brief recapitulation of what we know abo
our astronomical frequent occasi
to specify a distance in terms of the time it takes light to tra

62

Notes

In "On Air and Angels: The Numbers", the quote "John Donne, Anne Donne, un-done" was previously written by Donne.

"Table 2.1" is adapted from Willett Kempton's *Environmental Values in American Culture.*

"The Aether Notes" contains, with liberties taken, language and concepts from Andrew Worsley's essay "String quintessence and the formulation of advanced quantum gravity," which originally appeared in *Physics Essays.* It also contains an adapted line from Richard Hugo's poem "Lake Byron, Maybe Gordon Lord." Hugo's lines reads, "I don't know what water does to paper/ but it must be awful, like one human/ to another." Also, the line "My own myself" is borrowed from Tom Phillips's *The Humument.*

"[Transmigration]" alters lines from "Book 12" of *Paradise Lost* by John Milton.

"Array" contains adapted language and a borrowed image from Hannes Alfven's *Worlds-Antiworlds.*

Acknowledgments

The author would like to thank the editors of the following journals, in which some of the poems first appeared: *Best New Poets 2011, Mid-American Review, American Letters & Commentary, LVNG Magazine, The Meadow, The Offending Adam, Bayou Magazine, Word Riot, Word for/ Word, Slippery Elm, Zone 3, Peauxdunque Review,* and *Doubleback Review.*

Thank you, AB Gorham and Lisa Tallin, for your time, patience, and insightfulness, in this poetry and in all poetry. Thank you, Sonja G. Rossow, for collaborating with me and for finding a space for my work within your art. I am grateful to all my teachers, Peter Streckfus, Robin Behn, Joel Brouwer, Joanna Klink, Debra Magpie Earling, and especially my first teacher, Robert Stubblefield.

My eternal thanks to Christine E. Kelly, Laura Wetherington, Danilo John Thomas, and everyone at Baobab Press for your guidance and for your belief in this book.

To my family, of course, for supporting me, and to my partner, Keosha, for being there—you will get a poem someday.